Chess Book: How to Play Chess for Beginners: Learn Chess Today with a Short Primer of Chess Rules, Special Moves, and Fundamentals

By Allen Wilson

Welcome

Thank you for buying my ebook. I love playing Chess and showing other people how to play, so let's get started.

History

Before we learn Chess, let's begin with a little history.

The game we know as Chess started in India between 280 – 550 CE. It was originally called *Chaturanga,* which refers to *4 Divisions of the Military*, but the pieces and gameplay has changed immensely. It is the most widely played board game in the world with over 600 million players.

In popular culture, Chess is known as a game of wits, intellect, and calculation. Chess has produced several well-known figures, including Bobby Fischer, who was depicted in the movie *Searching for Bobby Fischer* as an eccentric genius. As of writing this, a Chess player named Magnus Carlsen is the reigning champion. He is one of the youngest Chess champions of all time.

People play Chess across the world from impromptu games in the streets and in homes to highly regulated tournaments. With its universal rules and low barrier of entry, Chess has the powerful ability to bring people together across social and economic boundaries.

Learning Objectives: Chess Rules and Fundamentals

In this book, we are going to start with the basic fundamentals, including the objective of the game, the names and starting locations of the pieces, how to move each piece, and how to checkmate.

After the basics, we'll cover basic Chess strategy, openings, tactics, and Checkmate patterns.

Let's begin.

The Chess Board

A Chessboard contains 64 alternating white and black squares. There are two players in Chess, each with 16 pieces. At the beginning of the game one player must choose to play with White or Black pieces, the other player uses the opposite color.

The player who chooses the White pieces moves first. Each player takes turns moving and each player may only play one turn at a time. A player may not choose to forfeit his turn; he *must* play when it is his turn.

The objective of the game is to checkmate the opponent's King. A checkmate is when the King is both under attack and cannot move to adjacent squares. We will cover checkmate in more depth when we discuss how to move the King.

Navigating the Board

In Chess, players use a system called algebraic notation to designate each square on the board. The columns are called Files and from left to right they are labeled A through H. The Rows are called Ranks and they are labeled 1 through 8.

To identify a certain square, one would first say the File followed by the rank. For example, if someone wants to identify the square in the bottom left corner, one would say a1. One would call the square in the top right corner h8.

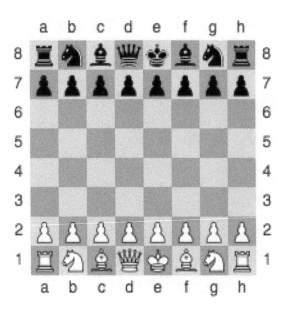

Setting up the Board

At the beginning of the game, the pieces are always set up the same. All Pawns are across the second rank. If you are playing White, your pieces from left to right are: Rook, Knight, Bishop, Queen, King, Bishop, Knight, Rook. For Black, the set up is the same except the King and Queen are switched. As you can see, Black's King is directly across the board from White's King.

We are going to discuss the pieces and their corresponding names in the next section, so don't worry if you don't know them yet.

When setting up the board, it's important to remember a white square is always on the near the right corner of the board. "White on the Right."

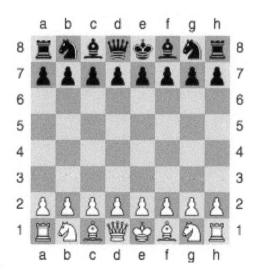

Pawns

The Pawn derives its name from the word *peon*. In terms of value, it is the least valuable piece because there are many more Pawns on the board than any other piece.

In general, a Pawn moves forward one space, but it can only take an opponent's piece if the piece is ahead of the Pawn diagonally. If a Pawn has not yet moved from the second rank, it can move two spaces forward.

The Pawn cannot move sideways or backward.

The Pawn is estimated to be worth 1 point and is often sacrificed to gain position in a strategic move called a "gambit."

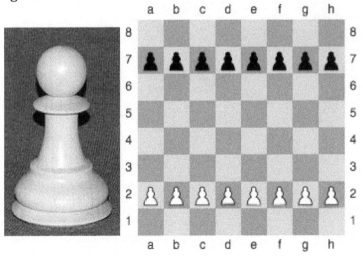

Bishop

The Bishop can move diagonally in any direction as many squares as can be allowed. It can take opposing pieces by moving diagonally onto the square. Contrary to the Knight it cannot jump over other pieces. The Bishop is estimated to be worth 3 points and is a great piece for pins and skewers.

Knight

The Knight is usually depicted as a horse. It is the only piece that can jump over other pieces. It takes an opposing piece by "jumping" onto the opposing piece's square and at the same time removing the opposing piece from the board. The Knight moves in an L-shape by moving two squares in any direction and then one square perpendicular. The Knight is also estimated to be worth 3 points.

Knights are perfect for a tactic called a fork, which will be discussed later.

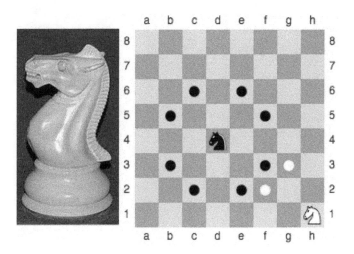

Rook

The Rook is depicted as a castle. It can move forward, backward, or sideways as many squares as possible, but it cannot jump over other pieces. It takes an opposing piece by moving onto the square of the opposing piece and removing the opposing piece from the board.

The Rook is the third most valuable piece, estimated to be worth 5 points. It is a key piece in a special move with the King called castling.

Queen

The Queen is a powerful piece estimated to be worth a whopping 9 points! The Queen can move forward, backward, left, right and diagonally in any direction, as many squares as can be allowed. She takes by moving onto an opposing piece's square and removing the opposing piece from the board.

Despite the Queen's dynamic moving ability, she cannot jump over other pieces, but she is still a critical piece in both offense and defense.

King

The King is the most important piece on the board. The game ends when one player's King is in checkmate. Like the Queen, the King can move in any direction: left, right, forward, backward, and diagonal. However, unlike the Queen, the King may only move a distance of one square per turn. The King takes an opposing piece by moving onto the opposing piece's square and removing that piece from the board.

The King does not have a value in points because the King is the objective of the game. If the King is checkmated, the game ends.

Check, Checkmate, and Illegal Moves

When an opposing player directly attacks a King, the player must say "check." Check is like saying "your King is under attack."

When a King is in check, the player must move the King out of check immediately. A player can move out of check in one of two ways. 1) By moving the King to another square where he is not in check. 2) By moving another piece in between the King and the checking piece that blocks its attack or by 3) taking the piece that is putting the King into check. In the image below, the black King is in check by White Queen..

When the King is in check and cannot move out of check using any of the three methods above, it is checkmate. The player whose King is checkmated loses.

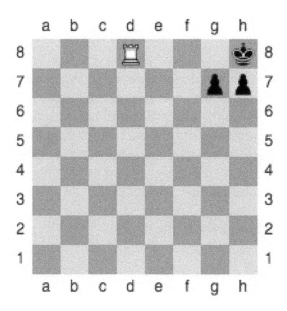

A player cannot make a move that puts his King into check. Such a move is illegal. If the player makes an illegal move, the player must move back to the last legal position and make a legal move.

Castling

Castling is a special move where a King moves toward a Rook of choice two squares and the Rook jumps the King to a square on the other side and adjacent to the King. However, castling cannot occur if the King or the Rook of choice have previously moved. Even if the Rook or the King have moved previously and moved back to their original squares, they cannot castle.

A King also cannot castle if
- He is in check
- Will pass through a square where he is in check
- Will castle onto a square where he is in check

Castling is an important offensive and defensive strategy.

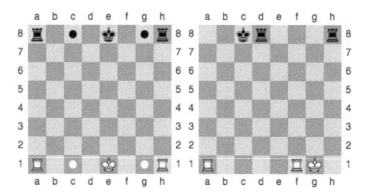

Other Special Moves: Promotion and En Passant

Besides Castling, there are two other special moves: Promotion and En Passant.

Promotion

Promotion is when you move your Pawn to the opposite end of the board. In this case, you can promote the Pawn to a Knight, Bishop, Rook, or Queen. It doesn't matter if you already have one of those pieces. You can even have double Queens. The promotion takes place after moving it onto the final square but within the same turn.

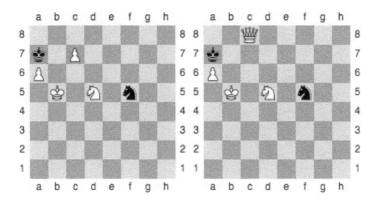

En Passant

En Passant is when an opponent's Pawn is two squares a way and diagonal to your Pawn that has not moved. If you move your Pawn two squares up, which is allowed only on the first move, the opposing Pawn has the option to take your Pawn off the board and move onto the diagonal square as if your Pawn has moved only one square. If the opposing player wants to make an en passant move, he must make it in the move immediately following the Pawn's initial two square move. This special moe is not common, but can be useful.

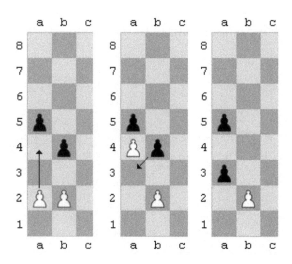

Chess Strategies and Chess Tactics

Now that you know how to move the pieces, let's discuss basic strategy and tactics.

Check and Re-check

Before you make each move, make certain you're not moving to a square where your opponent can take your piece. This may seem obvious but it is harder than it sounds. The less pieces you have, the harder it is to checkmate your opponent.

Devise a Plan

Develop a plan to attack your opponent's King and orchestrate all your pieces to follow that plan. The best plan to start with is an opening. We will discuss openings later in this book. The next plan you will need to come up with usually consists of a series of tactics in the middle and endgame, also discussed later.

Check for Safety

Make certain your King is safe at all times. You may have the best plan in the world, but if your opponent checkmates you, you lose the game.

This is basic advice for beginners, but it is extremely important. Next, let's talk about some more advanced strategy and tactics.

Control of the Center

The center is the four squares in the middle of the board.
You want to move your pieces to attack or control the
center of the board first. The center is shown by the X's
below.

In the example below, d4, e4, d5, and e5 are the center
squares. Both opponents are attempting to control the
center as they both have Black has a Queen in the center
and White has a Queen and two Knights pointed at the
center.

Develop, Develop, Develop

Hopefully saying develop three times will help you remember. Make sure you're moving your pieces out early, don't move only your Pawns. In the beginning of the game, you should focus on moving your Knights and Bishops out along with your Pawns.

You want to try not to move the same piece more than once.

In m opinion, the best first moves for beginners is either your D or E Pawns, followed by a Bishop or Knight.

In the image below, White has good piece development because he has a Pawn, and Knight, and a Bishop out.

Three Phases of a Chess Game

You can break a Chess game into three basic phases. The Opening, the Middle Game, and the Endgame.

The Opening is the first few moves where you're trying to control the center and develop your pieces.

The Middle Game is where you win your opponent's pieces and continue controlling the center.

The Endgame is where you organize and align your pieces to checkmate your opponent.

Chess Openings

Next, let's talk about ways to open the game.

The Ruy Lopez

The Ruy Lopez is a great opening for beginners. Its key feature is it pins the Knight on c6, usually leading to an exchange of the b5 Bishop and the c6 Knight.

The Italian Game

The Italian game is great for developing pieces, controlling the center, and developing an attack on Black's f7 square.

The King's Gambit

The King's Gambit aims to control the center by inviting one of Black's central Pawns to take a Pawn, which would lead it outside of the center. Giving up the Pawn is called a gambit. Ideally, White gives up the Pawn for better position.

Defensive Openings

The Caro-Kann Defense

Opens up the board for the Queen and prepares for Black's center Pawns to extend their reach into the center.

The French Defense

Protects the very fragile f7 square while allowing Black's other central Pawn to help control the center.

Middle Game

The Middle Game begins approximately when your pieces are fully developed and your King is protected. At this stage, positional play and tactics become an important focus of the game. There are three main types of tactics: Forks, Pins, and Skewers.

Forks

A Fork is when you attack two pieces at the same time. Forks can be accomplished with every piece, including Pawns and Kings. When you attack two of your opponent's pieces, your opponent must choose which piece to save, the other piece you take.

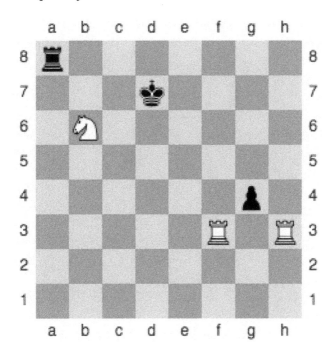

Pins

A Pin is when you freeze or pin one of your opponent's pieces between it and another of your opponent's piece of higher value. The King is usually the piece of higher value because moving the pinned piece would be illegal since putting your own King into check is not allowed.

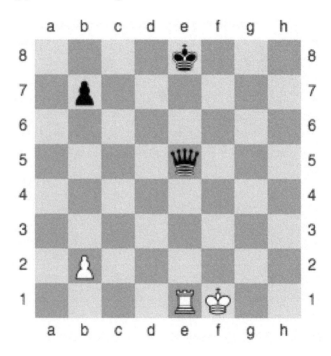

Skewers

A Skewer is when you attack two pieces (typically of higher value) through each other as if it's stabbing through them. For example, in the image below the White Bishop skewers a Queen and a Rook.

Endgame

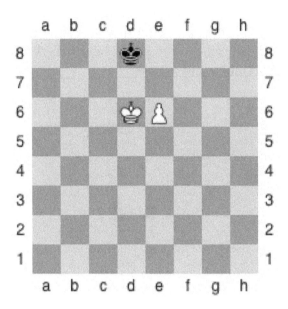

While early checkmates in the Middle Game and even the Opening are possible, checkmate typically occurs in the Endgame. Although checkmate is the most likely way the game will end, the game can end in the following ways.

Checkmate
Resignation
Forfeit
Draw
Stalemate

Let's discuss each of these options in the next pages.

Checkmate

The most likely result of the endgame is checkmate. Usually the side with the most pieces will eventually win. Remember, checkmate occurs only when the King is in check and cannot legally get out of check.

Here is a good example of checkmate. Notice how the Black King cannot move to b8, b7 because the two bishops are attacking those squares. The Black King also cannot move to a7 because the White King is attacking that square.

This checkmate is a common way to checkmate when only two bishops are left on the offense.

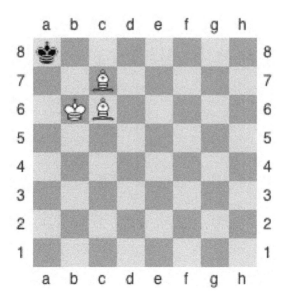

Using a King and Queen is another common way to checkmate.

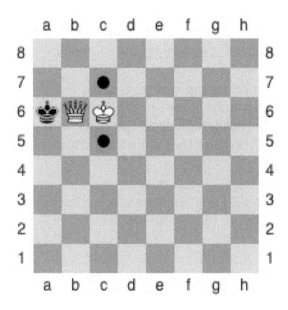

Resignation

When a player believes he cannot win the game, he may also resign. A resigning player loses the game.

The rules for resigning vary whether you're playing in a tournament or playing with a casual game with friends or family. In a tournament, you may need to say, "I resign." And, you may or may not have tip your King onto his side. Then, you may be expected to shake your opponent's hand. When you play among your friends it may be enough to simply tip your King over.

Forfeit

If a player breaks house or tournament rules, such as being late for a match or even if his phone rings during a game, a player may forfeit, losing the game.

Other violations include touching a piece without moving it, clock violations, or other methods of using illegal moves or cheating.

Draw

A draw (not to be confused with stalemate) is when no one wins the game. Draw can occur in a few ways.

Threefold repetition- When the exact same position occurs three times in a row, a player may claim a draw.

Fifty Move Rule – When no player has moved a Pawn and no captures have been made in 50 moves, a player can claim a draw.

Impossibility of Checkmate – When neither player can possibly checkmate the other, the game is automatically a draw. Usually this is the result of insufficient material, which is when the pieces on the board cannot possibly accomplish checkmate.

Mutual Agreement – Two players may also agree to a draw at any point in the game for any reason. Typically, this occurs when both players know the game will likely end in stalemate or if carrying out the game would take too long.

Insufficient Material – If any of the piece combinations below occur, the game is an automatic draw.

King vs. King
King and Bishop vs. King
King and Knight vs. King
King and Bishop vs. King and Bishop (if Bishops on the same color)

In the next pages, I will illustrate these different types of insufficient material.

Insufficient Material

King vs. King

Any game with only two Kings can only result in a draw. Because Kings cannot put themselves into check, no King can ever become close enough to another King to check him. Furthermore, even if it could (which it can't), the opposing King would always be able to escape. So, if you are playing a game where there is a King vs. a King, the game is a draw and it's over.

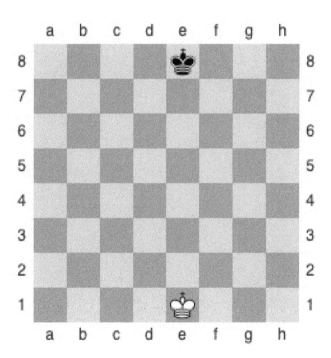

Insufficient Material

King and Bishop vs. King

A King and a Bishop is simply insufficient to cause checkmate against an opposing player. Because Bishops can only control diagonal squares their reach is extremely limited and not enough (even with the help of the King) to checkmate.

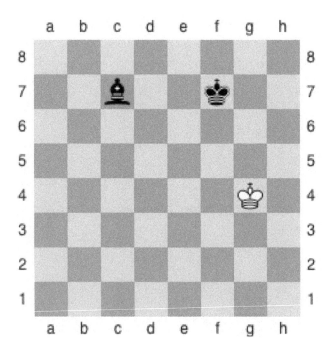

Insufficient Material

Bishop and King vs. Bishop and King

Similarly, a King and a Knight is also insufficient to checkmate against an opposing player. A Knight simply does not have the reach to assist in checkmating an opposing King.

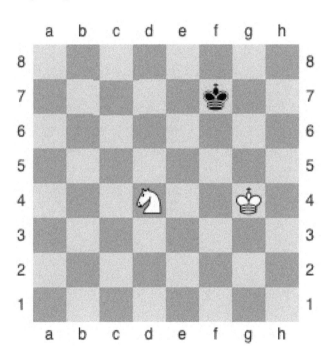

Insufficient Material

King and Bishop vs. King and Bishop (if Bishops on the same color)

Similar to Bishop and King vs. King. When two each side has a Bishop on the same-colored square, both sides have insufficient material to checkmate.

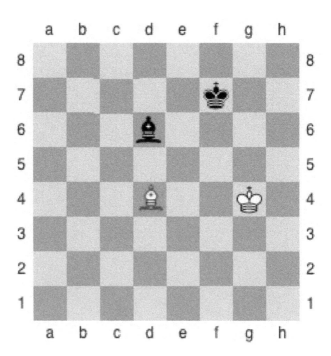

Stalemate

A Stalemate usually results in a draw (depending on the house or tournament rules), but by definition it is when one player is not in check and cannot move the King or any other piece without putting himself into check.

Below is an example of a stalemate. Notice neither White's King nor White's Queen are directly attacking the Black King. But, the Black King cannot move anywhere.

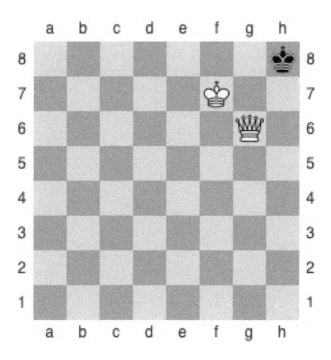

If this situation occurred in a game, the game would result in a draw and neither player would win. Notice that even though White has more pieces, it doesn't not mean White wins in the draw or stalemate.

Checkmate Patterns

At the end of the game, players usually have many less pieces on the board than when they started. In order to win the Endgame, you must be able to checkmate with the pieces you have.

The following are common patterns you can use to checkmate your opponent with certain pieces.

Back Rank Mate

The back rank mate usually occurs when a Queen or Rook moves to the Back Rank (or Back Row) of the opponent's side of the board. Typically, the King is blocked by two or more pawns, but could be block by any other pieces.

Notice that Black's King cannot move anywhere without being in check, and the two Black Pawns in front of him block him from moving anywhere.

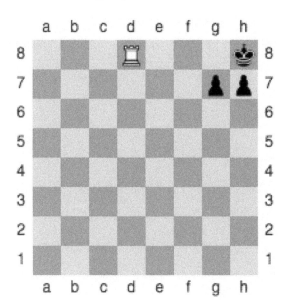

Damiano's Bishop Mate

Damiano's Mate is a good checkmate to know since it is a common endgame formation. While the image below shows Black's King being checkmated with by a Queen and protected by a Bishop. The piece protecting the Queen could easily be a Knight, a Rook, a Pawn or even a King.

Another key elements is that the Bishop is protecting the Queen. While it's counterintuitive to move your Queen into a place where she might be in danger, the smart Chess player knows how to protect his or her own pieces to achieve checkmate.

Smothered Mate

The Smothered Mate displays the true power of the Knight. What's great about this checkmate is its difficulty to predict because the Knight moves and attacks in an unusual way. While Black may have thought he was protected by surrounding himself with his own pieces, the Knight pierces through this defense by being able to jump or attack over other pieces.

Of course, this checkmate is so named because the King is "smothered" by his own pieces.

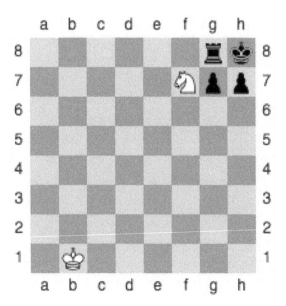

David and Goliath Mate

Referencing the old Bible story of David and Goliath, this checkmate is so-named because the little guy (the Pawn) delivers the final blow against the almighty King.

What's critical assisting this checkmate is the Rook blocking the entire 5th rank and the b2 Pawn preventing the King from escape. Black's other pieces also inadvertently assist in this checkmate.

Epaulette Mate

An Epaulette is a shoulder-piece typically worn by military officers. This checkmate is named the Epaulette Mate because the two Rooks beside the King act as "shoulder pieces" that box the King in, allowing the White Queen to simply stop two squares ahead for a checkmate.

In case you're curious, here's an image of an officer wearing epaulettes.

Box Mate (Rook Mate)

The Box Mate is similar to the Back Rank mate in that the Black King is trapped on one rank or file and that rank or file is being attacked by a lone Rook.

The difference here is that instead of being blocked by his own pieces, the Black King is being trapped onto the Back Rank by the opposing King.

Another difference is that this checkmate doesn't necessarily need to happen on the Back Rank. It could occur on either of the side files or even on the opposite (front) rank.

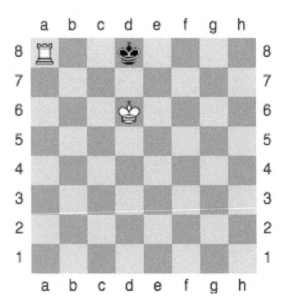

King and Two Bishops Mate

As Bishops are one of the pieces to likely to survive the game, it's critical to know a King and Two Bishops Mate. The hard part about check mating with Bishops is that they can't cover entire ranks or files, making it easy for an opposing King to squeeze past their range of attack. For example, with a Black squared Bishop the opposing King could easily move to a White squares.

But, with the two Bishops mate, you can effectively cover both black and white squares, while slowly moving pushing the King into a corner. With the help of the King, the two Bishops can trap the King into a corner, eventually delivering checkmate.

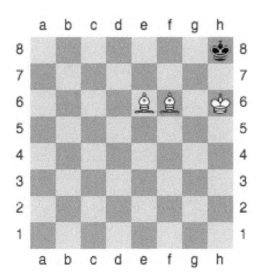

King and Two Knights Mate

Because the attack range of a Knight is much more spread out than other pieces, it may seem difficult to checkmate with a Knight or even two Knights. But it is possible. Again, the King is crucial in helping to deliver these checkmates. Essentially, White will use a King and a Knight to corner the opposing King and deliver the final below with the second Knight.

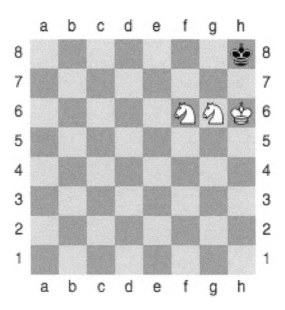

Arabian Mate

The Arabian Mate uses the Knight to protect the Rook and to block available squares from the Black King. The Rook delivers the final below, sealing the game.

King and Queen

This is one of the most common checkmates and it's critical to know. The key here is to use the Queen and her wide reach to move the opposing King into a corner or a side of the board. The King then comes in behind to help secure the border created by the Queen and to protect the Queen as she delivers checkmate.

This checkmate is similar to the Damiano's Bishop mate mentioned earlier - except this time the King is providing the protective support instead of the Bishop.

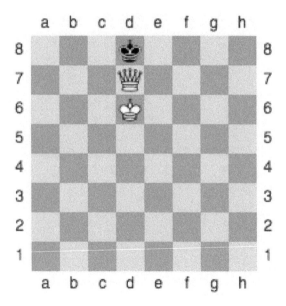

Checkmate Pattern Conclusion

You can play the best game in the world, but if you can't end the game with a checkmate pattern, it all may be for nothing.

Become familiar with these checkmate patterns and practice them. Eventually, you'll know how they look by heart and you will be able to execute them intuitively.

Glossary

We are nearing the end of the book. While I have shown you the most essential fundamentals of Chess, there is still a lot more to learn. The following are some lesser-known terms not covered in this book. One day, with practice and study, you too will know these terms and will be able to apply them in games.

Active
1. Describes a piece that controls a number of squares, or a piece that has a number of squares available for its next move.
2. An "active defense" is a defense employing threat(s) or counterattack(s).

Adjournment
Suspension of a chess game with the intention to finish it later. It was once very common in high-level competition, often occurring soon after the first time control, but the practice has been abandoned due to the advent of computer analysis. See *sealed move*.

Adjudication
Decision by a strong chess player (the **adjudicator**) on the outcome of an unfinished game. This practice is now uncommon in over-the-board events, but does happen in online chess when one player refuses to continue after an adjournment.

Battery
An arrangement of two pieces in line with the enemy king on a rank, file, or diagonal so that if the middle piece moves a discovered check will be delivered. The term is also used in cases where moving the middle piece will uncover a threat along the opened line other than a check.

Blindfold Chess
A form of chess in which one or both players are not allowed to see the board.

Building a Bridge
Making a path for a king in the endgame by providing protective cover against checks from line-pieces. A well-known example is the Lucena position.

Combination
A clever sequence of moves, often involving a sacrifice, to gain the advantage. The moves of the opponent are usually forced (i.e. a combination does not give the opponent too many possible lines of continuation).

Desperado
1. A piece that seems determined to give itself up, typically either to bring about stalemate or perpetual check.
2. A piece to sell itself as dearly as possible in a situation where both sides have hanging pieces.

Fool's Mate
The shortest possible chess game ending in mate: 1.f3 e5

2.g4 Qh4# (or minor variations on this).

Hanging
Unprotected and exposed to capture. It is not the same as *en prise* since a piece *en prise* may be protected. To "hang a piece" is to lose it by failing to move or protect it.

J'adoube (Touch-Move Rule)
[from French] "I adjust", A player says "J'adoube" as the international signal that he intends to adjust the position of a piece on the board without being subject to the touched piece rule.

Luft
[from German: *air*] Space made for a castled king to give it a flight square to prevent a back-rank mate. Usually *luft* is made by moving a pawn on the second rank in front of the king.

Pawn chain
A locked diagonal formation of pawns, each one supported by a friendly pawn diagonally behind and blocked by an enemy pawn directly ahead. Aron Nimzowitsch considered pawn chains extensively, and recommended attacking the enemy pawn chain at its base.

Prophylaxis
[adjective: prophylactic] Prophylactic techniques include the blockade, overprotection, and the mysterious rook move
1. A move that frustrates an opponent's plan or tactic.
2. A strategy in which a player frustrates tactics initiated by the opponent until a mistake is made.

Takeback
Used in casual games whereby both players agree to undo one or more moves.

Triangulation
A technique used in king and pawn endgames (less commonly seen with other pieces) to lose a *tempo* and gain the *opposition*.

Zeitnot
[German] Having very little time on the clock to complete the remaining moves of a timed game. Synonymous with time pressure.

Zugzwang
[German] When a player is put at a disadvantage by having to make a move; where any legal move weakens the position. Zugzwang usually occurs in the endgame, and rarely in the middlegame.

Zwischenzug
[German] An "in-between" move played before the expected reply. In general, this involves responding to a threat by posing an even bigger threat to the opponent, forcing him to respond to the threat first.

Conclusion

Chess is a complex and profound game. It can take hours or even minutes to learn, but a lifetime to master. I have enjoyed countless hours playing Chess with my family and others, and I hope you will too. With practice, you can use the Chess rules, fundamentals, and tactics in this book to beat your opponents.

Thank You

Thank you for purchasing and reading this book. If you enjoyed the book and you have a minute, will you leave a review for me? Simply return to the details page on Amazon and leave review.

Thank you and happy Chess playing!

Lightning Source UK Ltd.
Milton Keynes UK
UKHW041824290719
347033UK00001B/247/P

9 781729 466919